I Can't Breathe

I Can't Breathe

Poems by

Nancy Dillingham

Cover design by Shay Culligan

Cover art by Maggie Whitney "Meltdown 1"
www.maggiewhitneyart.com

Author photo by Bill Mosher

ISBN: 978-1-952326-97-4

Kelsay Books
502 South 1040 East, A-119
American Fork, Utah, 84003

Contents

. . . the moon is broken and the sky is cracked . . .
—Tom Waits

Hunkering Down

by order
of the governor

coronavirus
on the prowl

Disguised
wearing masks

we hold our breath
keep our distance

pray
for its demise

What to Look for in a Mask

(in the year of Pandemic)

Ask for the softest cloth. It will be useful
when your nose starts to itch and twitch
or when you cough. Request the boldest print,
one that will stop traffic, repel the coronavirus
and the pesky people who come too close.
Ask for one in red or gold covered in question marks
or the poignant word WHY? Or just request a black one
emboldened with skull and bones. Seek out the mask
with a giant crying eye. A word of advice: Avoid the shyster
who tries to sell you the economy-sized box of masks
stamped with the words "Open for business."

Things to Do while Sheltering in Place

Don't rant
Don't rave
Conjure a chimichanga
enchilada or souffle
Crave a cheesecake or chocolate
Make an omelette
Count calories
Go on a diet

Take a walk
Jog in place
Fly a kite
Order new pajamas
or a bed in a bag
Avoid crying jags
Keep a diary
or a dream journal

Don't condone violence
Eschew hate
the blues or bad news
Play your favorite music
Create a new "bored" game
Debate the universe
Memorize Hamlet's soliloquy
Recite "Jabberwocky"

Start a blog
Clean closets
Jettison junk
Write a letter of apology
to the last person you insulted
Tell someone you love them
Phone a friend
Practice yoga

Savor solitude
Watch the stars
Be brave
Pray every day
You are not alone

Bordering on Recluse

Among lettuce leaves
he twirls an imaginary mustache

dusts ash
from a celery stick

works his shtick
even gives her nose an "air" tweak

At the grocery store each week
perambulating abandoned aisles

she feigns pique
making a bee-line

for the produce display
seeking a peek

at the sly pantomime
of the green masked man

Murder in Minneapolis: May 25, 2020

The end of life has its own nature also worth our attention.
—Mary Oliver

Last night I watched fires
burning on the screen

Today I wake to see green
leaves turning in the breeze

recall teeming bodies
rioting on the streets

I pause to say a prayer
for George Floyd

who will never again feel
the wind blow and know

the freedom of release

An Open Letter to COVID-19

Sly operator
who do you think you are
invading our borders
coming like a thief in the night
upending our lives
sending chills up and down our spines?

Catlike and indiscriminate in your "kills"
you charmed us, harmed us
took our young and old
sullied our livelihood
left us defeated, depleted
isolated, alone

Forewarning: we survived the Great Depression
polio, the Cold War, Vietnam, AIDs and Ebola
so don't look away and don't rest easy
our eyes are upon you
One day our spirits will rise
and we will annihilate you

From a Distance

God is watching us, from a distance.
—Julie Gold

A tiny speck in the universe
known as the "united states"
looks quiet tonight
lights glittering like stars
but up close it is a battleground
scarred and stained

In the nation's capital
police in riot gear
spray tear gas and rubber bullets
Army trucks and soldiers
with guns and bayonets
invade the Lincoln Memorial

A military helicopter
designed to strike fear in enemy forces
flies low over treetops
gusts of air from its rotors
scattering peaceful protesters
for a photo op

A memorial for a black man
martyred by a knee on his neck
ends in 8 and ½ seconds of silence
symbolizing the amount of time
he lay helpless on the ground
suffocating and dying

A pandemic of hate
and racial divide
spreads like a virus
threatens to debase
and eradicate
the human race

Birthmark

American was born with a birthmark.
　　　　　　—Condoleezza Rice

Home of the brave

give me a world where the birthmark
has been blurred, obliterated

where greedy landowners
didn't crave slaves

where untold souls
didn't have their lives taken

on occasions
for picnics and parades

ice cream and baseball
souvenirs and photo ops

I long for a land where the words
of our own lady of the harbor

Give us your tired, huddled masses
yearning to breathe free

no longer ring hollow

Between 1882 and 1962 4,000 blacks lost their lives by lynchings.

Bunker

Here in the bunker
feels like home

no marchers
no noise

no reporters
no Pelosi

Here in the bunker
I can gloat

no Obama nor Romney
no "Sleepy Joe"

Here in the bunker
free of "dis-ease"

I can polish my tweets
do as I please

pose for photographs
for *Time* magazine

Here in the bunker
no enemies to be seen

Here in the bunker
I am king

There Is a Space

In memoriam: 2020

There is a space
where you were

a room
where you breathed

a place
vacant now

where you lived

When the sun rises
and the dew dries

it is my eyes
that move over the land

a world
arid and barren

unrecognizable
without you

Something Is Wrong

Mornings I awake
to birdsong
breathtaking sunrises
or fresh air after rain

All the while
a vague niggling
in my brain reminds me
Something is wrong

The warning resounds
like a gong
Something is wrong
Something is wrong

From the radio
NPR intones
the latest coronavirus stats
that land like a stone

then as if to atone
segues to a musical interlude
But I am not assuaged
dissuaded or deluded

Something is wrong
and I feel life
as we know it
slipping away

forever gone

After John Lewis

(1940-2020)

We are tasked
to take a knee

wear a mask
cast a ballot

stand up
for justice

make
good trouble

pray for freedom
and for peace

(Un)Convention(al)

Above the White House
just before midnight
fireworks explode

"Trump 2020" touts
an agitated acolyte

A phalanx of flags
red, white, and blue
stands in silent rebuke

Congregants unmasked
glad-hand and mug
for the cameras

while overhead
untold viruses float
in the fouled air

Battleground 2020

We are in a battle for the soul of a nation.
                                        —Joe Biden

In the taking of Belleau Wood
in 1918 courageous American forces
engaged in hand-to-hand combat
with fists, knives, and bayonets

Yet one hundred years later
fearing his hair might become disheveled
in the rain our Commander-in-Chief refrained
from visiting Aisne-Marne Cemetery

to commemorate 1800 heroic soldiers
who lost their lives in the bloody fight there
while his "suckers" and "losers" epithets
once again took our breath away

To Notorious RBG, with Love

You stared down death
five times
became icon-tough

Unable to find a job
as "a woman
a Jew and a mother"

you litigated
gender equality
and won

When asked
how many women
on the court

were enough
When there are nine
was your retort

Short in stature
you cast a long shadow
your legendary mettle

priceless

Rose Garden

A gathering of politicos
at the White House

introducing SCOTUS nominee
Amy Coney Barrett

spreads coronavirus
over the Rose Garden

infecting POTUS and FLOTUS
three senators and advisors

causing chaos in the government
leaving the electorate in limbo

Infected

We must love one another or die.
               —W. H. Auden

Medivacked to Walter Reed
Trump continued to tweet

took a joy ride outside
to greet his flock

Coptered home to the
people's house

he climbed the stairs
flung off his mask

posed for a photo op
left the world in shock

"Don't be Afraid of COVID"

became a refrain from Trump
as he recovered from the virus
shouted virally in his tweets

in his wheezing and coughing
through numerous interviews
one over an hour
if you can believe it

Don't be afraid of COVID
he coaxed and intoned
wheedled and whined

Don't be afraid of COVID
he preached and entreated
from his White House retreat

above the cheering crowds
longing for succor
but suckered to lose

his breath becoming
poisonous on their tongues
his words bitterest blood
in their mouths

In America, Post-Coronavirus

. . . everywhere, a faint seepage,
I smell death.
                    —Denise Levertov

I've used up all
my passes on crowded hospitals . . .

The rains came
and like a virus spread

made puddles of light
in the streets

seeping through houses
everything contaminated

the stench rising

The Fall: 2020

As broken leaves
shatter like glass
in the sun

and the world becomes
another country
ruled by brilliant death

a solitary walk
in the woods
becomes revelatory

when I—wary of the morrow—
spy just in my sight
dark-winged sorrow

unwinding
the long red ribbon
of joy

Biden Time

And hope and history rhyme.
    —Seamus Heaney

Voice quiet yet commanding
he repeats his mantra

a fight for the soul
of America

The message shakes the room
vibrates throughout the land

Hungry citizens devour his words
yearning for better days

somewhere in the future
after the coronavirus fades

and the nation
can breathe again

Remembering Van Gogh

1853-1890

. . . we take death to reach a star.
—Vincent van Gogh, in a letter to his brother Theo
10 July, 1888

Behind the barred windows of an asylum
he divined his *Starry Night . . .*

Against the swirling turbulence
a dark cypress towers over a town

its taper-like fingers flaming skyward

Beyond the scars and strife
and the chaos of the cosmos

the artist refined his credo

Art is to console those
who are broken by life

About the Author

Nancy Dillingham is associate editor for *Speckled Trout Review,* an online poetry journal. Her collection of poems, *Home,* was nominated for a 2010 Southern Independent Booksellers Alliance award (SIBA). Recent publications are *Like Headlines: New and Selected Poems* and the chapbook *Revelation.* She lives in Asheville, NC.